# Ultimate beginners guide for
# starters

Malcolm Ramsey V.

1

# Table of Contents

# CHAPTER ONE

## GUIDE TO ALCOHOL INKS

This guide will tell you the best way to begin liquor inks! It's ideal for amateurs, however has valuable data for everybody.

Assuming you love the vibe of conceptual liquor inks and need to make your own delightful works of art yet don't have the foggiest idea where to begin - I have you! I'll walk you through the nuts and bolts, similar to the materials required, various procedures, and how to begin a composition. I'll likewise go over fixing liquor inks, wellbeing insurances, and answer a few normal inquiries. Let's get down to business!

What are liquor inks?

Liquor inks are dynamic, quick drying inks that can be utilized to make staggering works of art on different non-permeable surfaces. These concentrated inks are liquor based and waterproof. They're hazy which implies they can be layered and consolidated together to make dazzling impacts. A liquid medium can be utilized in various ways. I love making unique impacts so that is the very thing that I'll show you here (in addition to it's the most straightforward method for beginning)!

## *Instructions to utilize liquor inks*

To put it momentarily, you use drops of liquor ink, isopropyl liquor, and an air source to move the inks around a nonporous surface (like Yupo paper). The liquor vanishes thus the inks dry quickly. This allows you to get exceptional impacts that absurd with different mediums. Presently, I'll direct you through the entire cycle in more detail...

Materials required for liquor ink workmanship

The initial 3 materials are all you truly need to get everything rolling, except I've included different things that may be fun or valuable. However, don't bother getting them all!

I've incorporated some partner connects to make it simple for you to find the materials I'm discussing, and assuming you buy through these connections it helps support me at no additional expense for you. Much obliged to you ahead of time!

Liquor inks

The primary thing! My number one brands are the accompanying:

1.　　Ranger by Tim Holtz Alcohol Inks - Lots of variety choices, and inks that uncover new tones when you weaken them with isopropyl liquor. Frequently sold in 3-variety packs, similar to these ones. This is perfect to begin with as the varieties will generally function admirably together.

2.　　Piñata Alcohol Inks by Jacquard - Bright, concentrated inks that stay extremely consistent with variety when weakened. A small amount makes an enormous difference, and it's enjoyable to combine the inks as one to make your own custom tones. Their metal ink is my #1 metallic ink of all time!

3. Copic Marker Ink Refills - A gigantic scope of variety choices. Can be difficult to tell which ones to get and they are not generally so thought as a few different brands. Yet, the scope of varieties is astounding!

While beginning you just need 2 or 3 tones. I like to pick essential tones and combine them as one to make my own shades. Custom tones are so amusing to blend, and it sets aside you cash as well.

# CHAPTER TWO

## ISOPROPYL LIQUOR/MIXING ARRANGEMENT

1.      This weakens and mix your inks, as Yupo paper by Legion is what I typically use, and I love it! It's an engineered, water-safe paper. It can have the downside of staining, so you can't clean it off later.

2.      Nara paper - an option in contrast to Yupo, that can be cleaned off.

3.      Ceramic tiles can be cleaned off and painted on over and over. Make a point to get coated, white

tiles for the best outcomes. They're ordinarily modest and can be found at numerous home improvement shops.

4.    Art Boards - I get mine from here and I love these as they can be cleaned off, and are so easy to sap over on the off chance that you need. Save 10% with code COYASAUCE (I get nothing from that except for I simply love these surfaces).

5.    The beyond fired mugs, bowls and so on

6.    Plastic acrylic spaces - Can be cleaned off. Gem of Swimming in Color makes loads of tomfoolery

shapes and they're not difficult to cover on and afterward tar up in the event that you need.

7. Tim Holtz Adirondack Alcohol Ink Cardstock - great little size to rehearse on toward the beginning. Something to move the inks (an air source)

You can begin simply allowing the inks to air dry, yet a ton of the tomfoolery begins when you move the inks with an instrument like a hairdryer. I don't prescribe utilizing straws because of the exhaust of the inks. On the off chance that you choose to attempt it, try to breathe in far away from your work of art, and ensure you're in a very much ventilated region, and don't do it for a really long time. Likewise, dampness can assemble in the straw from your breath and it might accidentally affect the artistic creation. So I suggest one of the choices beneath:

1. Hairdryer - A many individuals suggest this one however I haven't attempted it, I simply utilize an old one from a secondhand shop. Pick a frail, low wattage hairdryer for better control.

2.    Airbrush - I've never utilized one yet a few specialists love utilizing one.

3.    Air blower/dust bulb - The principal picture is an ink blower made for pushing inks around the page as opposed to utilizing a straw. The subsequent picture is what I for one use - a sauce crush bottle. I haven't attempted to ink blower so can't think about them however my sauce bottle appears to impeccably work. Well as to tidy up any spills. It permits you to get intriguing impacts and plans with regards to your compositions. It capabilities with liquor inks similarly you use water with

watercolors. What's the contrast between these choices?

Mixing Solution comprises of isopropyl liquor and other added fixings. It keeps inks brilliant and striking, and eases back the drying time a bit. Be that as it may, a lot less expensive option is 91% or close to 100% isopropyl liquor.

These have fundamentally a similar capability so you can manage with either. Sometime later you should explore different avenues regarding the two choices, yet to get everything rolling I recommend almost 100% isopropyl liquor. It's my most loved in light of the fact that it's less expensive and functions admirably. A surface to paint on (a substrate). Typical paper assimilates the ink immediately without giving now is the ideal time to move around and blend. So a non-permeable surface works best, as it gives the inks time to stream and to make exceptional impacts. The following are a couple of choices that function admirably.

### *Mixing Tools*

You can involve various apparatuses for mixing and making impacts, examples, and plans. You certainly needn't bother with this multitude of provisions to begin, however you could have some around the house as of now!

1.    Cotton Swabs are great for subtleties, adding little dabs of ink or cleaning little regions away.

2.    Tim Holtz® Adirondack® Alcohol Ink Applicator and little bits of felt. Add inks and a little isopropyl, and stamp on your page to make bright foundations for card making, and so on.

3.    Paper towels to smudge and eliminate areas of ink.

4.    Ranger Mini Ink Blending Tool

5.    Paintbrushes for moving the inks, and adding subtleties.

6.    Gloves so you can utilize your hands to move the inks.

## *Respirator Mask*

*To me this is a vital buy. I utilize the above 3M half face respirator, with natural fume cartridges. You can tap the picture in the event that you're intrigued. You could likewise utilize a full facial covering to be extra cautious, simply try to utilize natural fume cartridges. It could appear to be costly yet safeguarding your wellbeing is definitely worth the effort. Besides you get to feel like a cool dystopian person when you wear it (or is that just me?)

Assuming you stain or pitch your craft it comes in really convenient there as well.

### *Needle tip bottle*

Little accuracy instrument bottles are astounding for applying isopropyl liquor to the page and furthermore for blending your own custom tones. I can't recollect the specific ones I got yet they were like the page and furthermore for blending your own custom tones. I can't recall the specific ones I got however they were like these one.

## *Little dog cushion*

Retentive liner to cover and safeguard your work surface.

## *Paper towels*

To perfect as you go, wipe up spills, and clean region of your artwork if necessary.

## *Cover/old garments*

To shield your garments from spills and stains.

## Veiling liquid

To keep specific regions liberated from ink. Utilize an old brush or elastic tipped brush to apply the liquid, to try not to harm brushes.

Apply it to the page and permit it to completely dry. Then, at that point, paint over it with liquor inks and when that has completely dried, focus on the covering liquid to uncover the negative space beneath.

### Nitrile Gloves

To safeguard your skin and they let you utilize your hands to move the inks.

Beginning

Liquor inks are exceptionally thought so begin with a solitary drop and add more as you go. They're waterproof, so to weaken them and keep them moving use isopropyl liquor or mixing arrangement. From this point forward I'll just specify isopropyl as it's what I like, yet either will work. Make a point to cover your work surface with something to get any ink and isopropyl that spills over the edges of your composition. The main thing to do is attempt the inks and simply notice them.

1. To beginning you can add one drop of ink to your page and watch what occurs... Nothing much. It fans out a bit and afterward dries rapidly.

2.    You'll before long need to zest things up with some isopropyl liquor, so add a drop of it right on top of the dried ink. The ink 'awakens' and begins moving. This is one of the great properties of liquor inks-they can be reactivated with isopropyl, allowing you to make layered, unique pieces that continue to change as you work on them.

3.    Experiment with adding a drop of isopropyl liquor and afterward a drop of ink, and afterward add one more drop of ink. See how the tones collaborate and move. You'll see that adding a second drop of ink can uproot the

main drop. I regularly put isopropyl liquor on the page first, and afterward add a drop of ink onto that puddle. It implies there's less possibility staining the page, and it begins moving immediately. You'll get the most enchanted impacts when you keep the inks liquid and moving with bunches of isopropyl, and significantly less ink. A tiny amount truly makes a remarkable difference and you can add more as you go. Use a lot of isopropyl to weaken colors and get straightforward and layered impacts.

# CHAPTER THREE

## EVALUATE VARIOUS APPARATUSES

I regularly join various devices and strategies in each work of art, however to find out about how you can manage various apparatuses.

### *Gravity*

Add isopropyl liquor and a couple of drops of ink to frame a puddle on the page. Get the paper and slant it around and watch what works out. Add a drop of another variety and perceive how they blend when you slant the page. At the point when you're cheerful, put it down to air dry. Or on the other hand you can begin keep dealing with it with a paintbrush...

## Utilizing Paintbrushes

They frequently lead to a somewhat more finished look. Have a go at painting ink and isopropyl onto a wet page. Then when it dries, take a stab at painting on top of it... The impacts are really unique! Utilize a touch of isopropyl to eliminate ink - and get a negative space impact like the moon above. Flick the brush against your hand to splash ink or isopropyl onto the page to get little dabs. Simply take the path of least resistance and sort out what happens when you attempt new things! Utilize an old/modest brush in light of the fact that the liquor will dry out the fibers.

## *Utilizing a Hairdryer*

This is my outright most loved device and air source to utilize. At first it will feel like the inks have their very own psyche and fly all around the page, so show restraint. Get going holding the hairdryer very distant from the page, and watch it move the ink. Attempt gradually bringing it closer, and move it around the page so it pushes the ink.

On the off chance that you continue to move the hairdryer around the puddle of ink all around, you'll begin to get a boundlessness ring impact. On the off chance that you move it around the page indiscriminately the inks will continue to move every which way, and you'll get a cool dynamic impact. As the inks dry, continue adding isopropyl to keep them streaming. Each hairdryer is different so the most effective way to learn is practice.

### Utilizing an Ink Blower

You can get astonishing impacts utilizing an ink blower - it works much the same way to utilizing your breath/a straw, however it's more secure and doesn't influence mugginess. Shared benefit! You can utilize it to direct the inks where you need to go, make blurs, mix tones, and so forth.

You can work with each little puddle in turn to get delicate blurs and different impacts. To do this I drop on some isopropyl, move it with the ink blower, and afterward drop ink on the edge of this puddle. Then, at that point, I utilize the air blower to push the ink part way into the isopropyl, so it shapes a blur.

You can likewise put a major puddle of isopropyl and inks all around the page and move them around and mix them, utilizing gravity and the ink blower, as in the photograph above. Go crazy!

I've recommended a couple of procedures so you can attempt various things and see what works for you. In any case, the most effective way to improve and learn is to get a decent grip on things. Explore allll the time, seek clarification on some pressing issues, make a monstrous wreck and have a great time. You'll foster your own belongings and one of a kind strategies, and that is the most thrilling sensation of all!

# CHAPTER FOUR

## WELLBEING SAFEGUARDS

1.    Store materials far away from pets and kids.

2.    Work in a very much ventilated region and adhere to all wellbeing guidelines for the materials you use.

3.    Alcohol inks and Isopropyl Alcohol/Blending Solution are combustible so avoid fire or intensity.

4.    Do not use isopropyl liquor in a shower bottle as it ought not be airborne.

5. Read the wellbeing information sheets for your materials. For instance here is the Ranger liquor ink mixative sheet. Seeing it like that makes me so happy I wear a respirator.

6. Wear a respirator veil! At the point when I began I simply needed to test liquor inks out, and for a couple of months I utilized no security gear. I was hesitant to wear a respirator as I once in a while utilized my breath to move the inks, however at that point I began getting migraines. I did some examination and got a respirator - and the cerebral pains disappeared! So presently I

(almost) consistently wear mine, and I love it... I like to drink liquor in a wine glass as opposed to breathe in it into my lungs. Consider the possibility that you can't manage the cost of a respirator yet, or simply need to evaluate liquor inks. By and by, I feel OK working without a respirator for brief timeframes, in a very much ventilated region. I'm sharing this for educational purposes just, this isn't clinical guidance or anything - Please do your own examination and settle on your own decisions! Primarily, you know the dangers and play it safe.

# CHAPTER FIVE

## FIXING YOUR SPECIALTY

Liquor inks are light delicate and will blur with time with openness to UV light. So I suggest you generally seal your completed works. Many stains are liquor based and would reactivate the inks and possibly ruin your work, so coming up next is my interaction. This works for me yet go ahead and change it to your necessities. In the event that you can't get to this brand, attempt to find a water based stain/fixative so it doesn't reactivate your inks.

## Stage 1: Krylon Kamar Varnish

Hold on until your specialty is totally dry (something like 24 hours to be protected). Place your craft inside a cardboard box and head outside/to a very much ventilated region, and wear your respirator cover. Splash it with around 3 layers of Varnish, holding up 15 minutes between coats. Cover the container between layers to ensure no residue lands on the workmanship as it dries.

## Stage 2: Krylon UV shower

Subsequent to staining I hang tight for a couple of hours or short-term. Utilize a similar stage 1 set-up. Then, at that point, splash with 1-2 layers of UV shower and pass on it to dry for somewhere around two hours. Your specialty is fixed! It's prepared to outline, or to cover with gum.

## Stage 3 (Optional): Resin

This is a further developed choice as the need might arise to realize about another medium. Numerous craftsmen love involving sap as a last coat since it gives a beautiful shiny completion. There are many brands out there to suit precisely exact thing you really want. My most loved is ArtResin for wall workmanship. I love Counter Culture DIY Artist Resin as well, particularly for liners, as it's more intensity safe when relieved.

# CHAPTER SIX

## FAQ AND TROUBLESHOOTING

I trust these response your inquiries! These are simply founded on my insight so I urge you to do your own examination :)

Might you at any point paint on material? Indeed, however as it's permeable inks will act contrastingly and may ingest into it rapidly. To further develop this you can prepare. I haven't done this, however I realize a many individuals prescribe that you use

Kilz2 to set up the material. It's a plastic groundwork found in tool shops where paint is sold. At the point when I utilize locally acquired material they ordinarily come pre-prepared with gesso, and I essentially paint on them right out of the pack. The inks move distinctively however getting stunning effects is as yet conceivable! How would you utilize liquor inks with tar? I ordinarily use sap to seal my artistic creations, yet it tends to be utilized in alternate ways as well. You can utilize liquor inks to color tar various varieties, or you can drop them straight into fluid pitch for a Petri dish impact. When a sap painting has restored you can likewise ink on top of the dried pitch, making a layered impact, which is something I love to do. While fixing with pitch is it important to stain prior to adding the gum? Assuming I'm making anything to sell I generally seal with heaps of stain and UV assurance to make the best work of art conceivable. In any case, in the event that you're simply exploring different avenues regarding something for yourself, there's no mischief in attempting. I've tried adding Art Resin onto unlocked workmanship and it functioned admirably, with a slight distinction in the metallic yet the rest looked fine. Ensure the work of art dries for basically several days prior adding sap. Results might rely upon the brand of inks and tar that you use.

# CHAPTER SEVEN

## ARE LIQUOR INKS FOODSAFE

I don't suggest utilizing them on any surface that will contact food, as it's not demonstrated food safe. Might you at any point paint on mugs and different dishes? Indeed, you can paint on porcelain for example mugs, adornments dishes, tile napkins, bloom jars, and so on. A white surface works best as the inks are straightforward. It very well may be trying because of the bended state of numerous porcelain things, so painting on them may be simpler in the event that you grasp the dish and turn it continually, to assist with controlling the inks. Some tolerance and practice will make it simpler! It should be fixed here and there as well and remember that fixatives regularly utilized with liquor inks are not foodsafe. For mugs, try to keep a hole between the inks and the edge of the mug. Are there options in contrast to Krylon Kamar Varnish and UV Spray?

Many stains are liquor based and would reactivate the inks and possibly ruin your work. On the off chance that you can't get to this brand, attempt to find a water based stain/fixative so it doesn't reactivate your inks.

# CHAPTER EIGHT

## ARE LIQUOR INKS RISKY

With the right precautionary measures I believe they're protected. Peruse the wellbeing information sheets of the items you use and make a point to wear a respirator and gloves if conceivable. I read this article at one point and it made me really happy I wear a respirator veil. I likewise composed a part on wellbeing safety measures. Might you at any point draw on top of liquor inks?

Indeed, simply ensure the inks are completely dried first. Posca pens are a famous decision, as are Sakura Gelly Roll pens and Microns. I can't get swells and slight lines! For straightforward impacts or flimsy, fragile lines, weakened inks work better. Scarce differences seem when the ink dries on the edge of the puddle of isopropyl. So focus on the state of the puddle of Isopropyl and you will actually want to anticipate and control where you'll get particular lines. To get fresh lines I have more karma with a warm air source.

Could you at any point make your own liquor inks? Indeed, this is the kind of thing I've done. You can make research on it. For what reason does my white liquor ink act so peculiarly? Jacquard Piñata Blanco is known to shock individuals by transforming into a thick, sticky wreck when utilized with isopropyl liquor. For what reason does this occur? Jacquard Piñata inks are ethanol based as opposed to isopropyl based. The white particularly doesn't work with Isopropyl Alcohol since it's less dissolvable in Isopropyl, so assuming you add that it can coagulate. If you have any desire to utilize white, try not to blend in with different brands like Ranger. Try to shake it a ton, and just use mixing arrangement with it and you ought to have more achievement. For what reason are my liquor inks getting all grainy and finished on the page? There could be a couple of explanations behind this. In the event that you're utilizing Jacquard Piñata inks, they are ethanol based and when utilized with isopropyl liquor it can diminish the solvency of the colors (particularly with hazier tones). The color can wind up isolating and turning out to be little bits of color on the page.

Here and there dampness can likewise prompt this kind of impact. I don't have the foggiest idea what variety inks to purchase? Help! Loads of specialists make samples of their inks and liberally share them. Where could I at any point buy supplies? Your nearby expressions and specialties store, or on the web. In USA my number one spots to shop were:

- Creation

- DeSerres

- Amazon

Best of luck on your craft process!

Much thanks to you for perusing and I trust you're amped up for being on this liquor ink venture. Have some good times and continue testing and attempting new things!

THE END